Contents

 Where you see this symbol, adult supervision is required.

Get ready to cook!

Cooking is a really good hobby. It's creative, it's fun – and you can eat the end result! It is also a great way of discovering different tastes and flavours, and what you do and don't like.

No-cook cooking... Sometimes!

This book is about cool food for spring. Many of the recipes need no cooking at all, while some will need time on a hob or in an oven.

The tangy 'Dip 'n' dunk' (pages 10-11) needs no cooking, but the 'Yummy, squidgy chocolate cake' (pages 28-29) would be extremely squidgy and not-at-all yummy if it wasn't baked in an oven! So, when you do use a cooking appliance, make sure an adult is with you and that oven gloves are at hand. Cool food is usually eaten cold, so these recipes would make great picnic snacks and lunchbox treats.

More than cool – crucial!
Food is really important – it gives you the energy to do all the things you love to do.

Food is fuel for your body. It keeps you moving and provides the energy for your growth and development. The best way to keep yourself healthy is to eat lots of different types of food so that you take in lots of different vital vitamins and nutrients.

You won't be healthy or happy if you eat only cake, or if you just eat carrots. One might make you fat; the other might, after a long time, turn you orange! But together, with a variety of other foods, they will keep you healthy and happy.

'Treats to Make and Bake' is brimming with recipes that are easy to prepare and cook, use lots of simple ingredients, and better still, taste and look great! But before you get started, read the 'Top ten tips' (pages 30-31) to help you become an ace chef!

 Where you see this symbol, adult supervision is required.

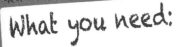

What you need:

250 grams strawberries

1 small banana

150 millilitres very cold milk

2 tablespoons strawberry yoghurt

1 tablespoon sugar, honey or maple syrup

OTHER SMOOTH FRUIT COMBINATIONS

peach and raspberry

passionfruit and mango

1 Remove stalks from the strawberries and halve any large strawberries.

2 Peel the banana and slice it into thick rounds.

3 Put the fruit, milk, yoghurt and sugar into a blender. Whiz together until thick and smooth. If you don't have a blender, chop the fruit finely, then push it through a sieve (the back of a ladle makes this easy) set over a plastic bowl. Add the milk, yoghurt and sugar to the fruit 'sauce' and stir well.

4 Taste the smoothie. Add more sugar, honey or syrup if the fruit needs sweetening.

5 Pour smoothie into glasses and enjoy this healthy drink now!

Breakfast
smoothie

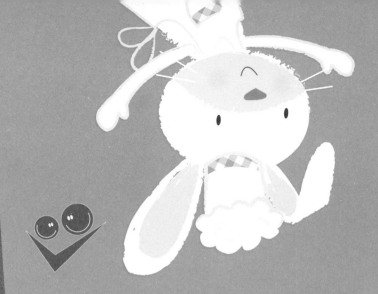

What you need:

12 tablespoons muesli

200 millilitres fruit juice

plain or fruit yoghurt

blueberries, raspberries or strawberries

WINTER FRUIT MUESLI

Spoon cooked fruits like apples, rhubarb and plums onto your muesli in place of fresh berry fruits in winter. It's so yummy!

1   Put the muesli into a medium-sized mixing bowl. Pour over the juice and mix gently. Cover the bowl and leave for 5 to 10 minutes. The muesli will soften and soak up the juice.

2   Spoon the muesli and juice mixture into four cereal bowls and top with the yoghurt and washed fruit.

3   To save time in the morning, combine the muesli and fruit juice the night before and leave the bowl covered in the refrigerator. In the morning, pour a little fruit juice over the mixture and stir.

Fruity muesli

What you need:

Mini muffin tins and 18 mini paper cases

50 grams butter

150 grams plain flour

2 teaspoons baking powder

50 grams caster sugar

50 grams ready-to-eat dried apricots, cut into small pieces

2 tablespoons sultanas

1 large egg, beaten

150 millilitres buttermilk or natural yoghurt

1 Preheat oven to 200ºC or gas mark 6. Line the muffin tins with paper cases.

2 Melt the butter in a saucepan, or in a bowl in the microwave. Leave to cool.

3 Sieve the flour and baking powder together into a mixing bowl and stir in the sugar. Add the apricots and sultanas and stir in well.

4 Beat together the melted butter, egg and buttermilk or yoghurt.

5 Pour the buttermilk mixture onto the dry ingredients. Mix lightly using a large metal spoon and a chopping action.

6 Spoon the mixture into the paper cases. Ask an adult to bake the muffins for 15 to 18 minutes, or until the muffins are golden brown and firm to the touch. Leave muffins to cool before eating.

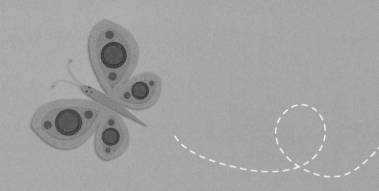

Mini muffins

What you need:

200 grams fromage frais

250 grams Cheddar cheese, grated

2 spring onions

227-gram can pineapple pieces

salt and pepper

paprika

carrot, pepper and celery, cut into sticks for dipping

crisps or corn chips

1 Beat the fromage frais in a mixing bowl with a wooden spoon, then add in the cheese.

2 Trim the ends of the spring onions and peel off the outer layer. Chop the spring onions into small pieces.

3 Drain the juice from the pineapple pieces. Chop the pineapple pieces into even smaller pieces.

4 Stir the onion and pineapple into the fromage frais mixture. Add salt and pepper until it tastes just right for you.

5 Pile the mixture into a small bowl and sprinkle with a little paprika.

6 Arrange vegetable sticks and crisps around the dip and prepare for some delicious dipping and dunking.

Dip 'n' dunk

What you need:

250 grams dried pasta shapes

salt and pepper

410-gram can kidney beans

1 carrot, peeled

1 green pepper, core and seeds removed

150 grams Edam cheese, wax removed

4 tablespoons natural yoghurt

6 tablespoons mayonnaise

small bunch fresh parsley

1 Fill a large pan with cold water and add a pinch of salt. Ask an adult to bring the water to the boil and add the pasta. Cook the pasta as directed on the packet.

2 Ask an adult to test if the pasta is cooked and also to drain the pasta into a colander set in the kitchen sink. Leave the pasta to cool.

3 Tip the kidney beans into a sieve and rinse them under cold, running water. Leave the beans to drain.

4 Chop the carrot, green pepper and cheese into small squares or dice.

5 Mix together the yoghurt and mayonnaise in a large serving bowl. Add the pasta, beans, and chopped vegetables and cheese. Sprinkle on salt and pepper to taste.

6 Finely cut or chop the parsley leaves and stir into the pasta. Serve with a fresh, green salad.

Pasta, please!

What you need:

4 large, fresh flour tortillas

120 grams cream cheese

150 grams hummus

1 carrot, peeled and grated

1 red and 1 green pepper, chopped into very small pieces

sweet chilli sauce (optional)

It's a wrap!

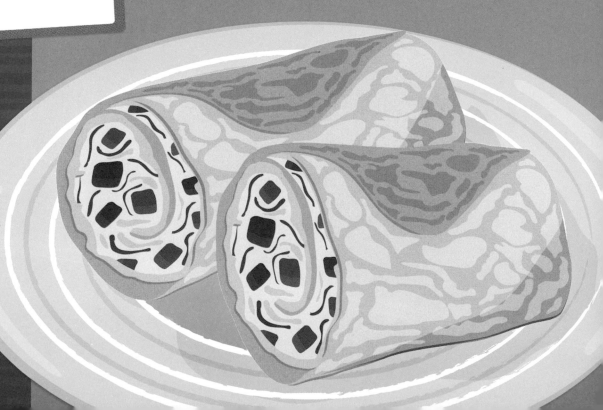

1 Lay the tortillas out on a clean, dry worktop. Divide the cream cheese into four and spread evenly over each tortilla. Make sure you spread it right to the edges.

2 Lightly spread the hummus over the cream cheese.

3 Mix together the carrot and peppers in a small bowl, and then sprinkle evenly over the hummus.

4 Roll up one tortilla and then wrap it in plastic food wrap. Roll and wrap the other three tortillas in the same way. Place on a plate in the refrigerator for one hour.

5 Remove the food wrap and trim the ends off each tortilla. Slice each tortilla into 8 to 10 pieces for a snack to share, or leave whole for an individual meal. Serve the wraps with a sweet chilli sauce if you like things spicy!

What you need:

500 grams new potatoes, washed

salt

4 frankfurters or vegetarian frankfurters

handful chopped fresh chives

30 seedless green grapes

6 tablespoons vinaigrette or salad dressing

1 Cut any large potatoes in half.

2 Ask an adult to bring a large pan of salted water to the boil and to add the potatoes to the pan. Cover the pan and leave to boil for 10 minutes. Ask an adult to test if the potatoes are cooked. They need to be tender, not mushy!

3 Put a colander in the kitchen sink and ask an adult to drain the potatoes. Run cold water over the potatoes to stop them cooking. Let the potatoes cool for 10 minutes.

4 Cook the frankfurters following the directions on the packaging.

5 Cut the potatoes and cooked frankfurters into bite-size chunks and put into a serving bowl with the chives and grapes.

6 Pour on the dressing and toss carefully so that every mouthful is covered with tangy dressing.

Frankfurter and potato shake

What you need:

1 cup easy-cook rice

1 teaspoon salt

1 red and 1 yellow pepper, seeds and core removed

1 carrot, peeled

3 spring onions, trimmed

5 tablespoons seedless raisins

DRESSING:

3 tablespoons olive oil

1 tablespoon white wine vinegar

1 teaspoon sugar

1 teaspoon French mustard

1 clove garlic, crushed

salt and pepper

1 Ask an adult to help with this recipe. Put the rice into a large saucepan with 2 cups of cold water and the salt. Place pan on the stove, turn up the heat and bring to the boil. Stir once, then cover pan with a lid. Turn down the heat and cook rice slowly for 12 to 15 minutes, until all the water has gone. Take off the stove. Leave covered for 5 minutes.

2 Make the dressing while the rice is cooking. Whisk all the ingredients together in a small bowl. Taste, then stir in extra salt and pepper or more sugar.

3 Spoon the hot rice into a large bowl, pour on the dressing and mix gently. Leave for 15 minutes.

4 Cut the peppers into thick slices and trim the ends off the peeled carrots. Trim the salad onions and peel off the outer layer. Chop all the vegetables into small pieces.

5 Add the vegetables and raisins to the rice and mix gently. Pile the Harlequin rice into a bowl and serve.

Harlequin rice

What you need:

5 tablespoons mayonnaise

250 gram tomato salsa, jar or fresh

200 grams cold cooked chicken (no skin) or cooked tofu fillets

1 stick celery, sliced

1 avocado

salt and pepper

spinach or lettuce leaves

Salsa chicken salad

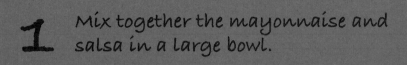

1 Mix together the mayonnaise and salsa in a large bowl.

2 Tear or cut the chicken or tofu fillets into bite-size pieces.

3 Cut the avocado in half lengthways and twist to separate the halves. Ask an adult to remove the stone.

4 Use a teaspoon and scoop out chunks of avocado and add them to the mayonnaise mixture.

5 Gently stir the chicken and celery into the mayonnaise mixture. Season with salt and pepper.

6 Cover a serving plate with spinach or lettuce leaves and spoon on the Salsa chicken salad. Serve this dish with the Harlequin Rice (pages 18-19).

What you need:

- 1 ciabatta loaf or small French stick
- 125 grams cream cheese
- 200-gram can tuna, drained
- 6 tablespoons canned sweetcorn
- 3 tablespoons mayonnaise
- lettuce, rocket, spinach or tasty watercress leaves
- 2 tomatoes, sliced

1 Check if the ciabatta needs baking before it can be used. Bake if necessary.

2 Cut the bread lengthways into two slabs. Spread cream cheese over the cut surfaces of the bread.

3 Fork the tuna into a bowl and mix in the sweetcorn and mayonnaise.

4 Spread the tuna mix over one half of the bread. Lay on lettuce leaves and tomato slices. This is a really huge sandwich, so pile on the goodies.

5 Pop the other half of the bread on top and push down firmly. Cut the Tuna mega-munch into 4 pieces or eat the whole thing yourself!

Tuna mega-munch

What you need:

- 1 eating apple
- 12 seedless grapes
- 125 grams blueberries
- 1/2 lemon
- 1 banana
- 1 orange
- 1 kiwifruit
- 425-gram can mango slices
- 10 Cape gooseberries (optional)
- 250 millilitres orange juice

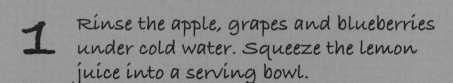

1 Rinse the apple, grapes and blueberries under cold water. Squeeze the lemon juice into a serving bowl.

2 Cut the apple into quarters and ask an adult to remove the core. Slice the apple and banana, and add to the bowl. Toss the fruit in the lemon juice.

3 Peel the orange and divide into segments. Peel the kiwifruit and drain the juice from the mango. Cut these fruits into bite-size chunks and add them to the serving bowl.

4 Pull the papery covers off the Cape gooseberries and add the gooseberries, grapes and blueberries to the bowl.

5 Cover the bowl with plastic food wrap and place in the refrigerator. It will keep for 2 days. Pour on the orange juice just before serving.

Fruitastic salad

What you need:

250 grams fresh or defrosted raspberries

4-6 tablespoons icing sugar

3 fresh peaches or 6 canned peach halves

vanilla ice cream

OTHER FRUITY IDEAS
strawberries, blueberries, stoned cherries, passion fruit or mango. Add extra sugar if needed and sieve the sauce to remove pips!

1 Whiz the raspberries and sugar in a blender, or push the fruit through a sieve with the back of a ladle, to make a thick sauce.

2 Pour the sauce into a sieve over a bowl. Press it through the sieve to remove the pips.

3 Chop the peaches into bite-size chunks and spoon into four tall glasses or sundae dishes. If using fresh peaches, toss the cut fruit in lemon juice first.

4 Pile scoops of ice cream onto the peaches.

5 Smother the peaches and ice cream with lots of sauce. Top your sundae with frothy cream if you like!

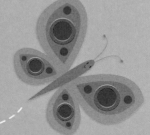

Ice cream sundae everyday

What you need:

2 20-centimetre sandwich tins and 200ml measuring cup

DRY INGREDIENTS:

1 cup self-raising flour

1 cup caster sugar

4 tablespoons cocoa

1/2 teaspoon salt

2 teaspoons baking powder

WET INGREDIENTS:

1 cup mayonnaise

1 cup cold water

1 teaspoon vanilla essence

ICING:

200 grams full-fat cream cheese

200 grams milk chocolate, broken into squares and melted

FILLING:

5 tablespoons apricot jam

1 Preheat the oven to 180°C or gas mark 4. Lightly butter the sandwich tins and cut a circle of baking parchment to line the base of each tin.

2 Mix the dry ingredients, then sieve the mixture two times into a large bowl.

3 Whisk the wet ingredients together in a small bowl.

4 Mix the wet mixture into the dry, and beat well until really smooth. Divide the mixture between the two tins.

5 Ask an adult to place the tins into the oven to bake for 30 minutes. To test if cooked, ask an adult to insert a skewer into each cake. If the skewer comes out clean, the mixture is cooked. Turn cakes out onto a wire rack to cool.

6 To make the icing, beat the cream cheese until soft, then beat in the melted chocolate. Sandwich the cakes together with jam and half of the icing. Spread the top of the cake with the remaining icing.

Yummy, squidgy chocolate cake

Top ten tips for

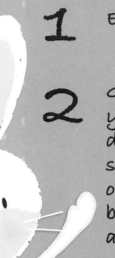

1 Enjoy yourself!

2 Get into washing your hands big time. Wash your hands when you start preparing food and during the cooking when hands have become sticky or you have been handling uncooked fish or meat. Make sure everything you use – dishes, bowls, tools and cutting boards, for example – are also clean.

3 Wear an apron to protect your clothes and to look like an ace chef. An apron is also the perfect thing for dabbing away sticky messes from fingertips!

4 Top chefs get all the ingredients prepared and chopped before they start cooking. They do this to double-check that they have everything and so that they can concentrate on the creative bit – the cooking.

5 Clear up as you go. This means that you will be able to enjoy what you have prepared as soon as

budding chefs!

it is ready. It is very boring to be washing up while an ice cream sundae waits to be eaten.

6 Sharp knives are safe if used with great care. Always ask an adult to help you. Hold a knife by its handle, blade pointing down, and carry it at your side.

7 When using pans on the hob, handles must be turned inward.

8 Never leave knives or dangerous kitchen tools, hot pots or uncooked foods within reach of younger children.

9 Always ask an adult to help you and use oven gloves when handling pans from the hob or dishes and tins from the oven or microwave.

10 Always ask an adult for permission to use the kitchen. In return, the adult will be on hand to help with hot pans and dishes, to check if a mixture or ingredient is fully cooked and, maybe even, to do some of the washing up!

Recipes and accompanying text: Rosemary Moon

Cover and content illustrations: Sarah Wade

Published by Autumn Publishing
A division of Bonnier Media Ltd
Chichester, West Sussex, PO20 7EQ, UK.

© 2011 Autumn Publishing Ltd

Printed in China